DATE DUE

APR 0 2 2001		
APR 3 0 2001		
MAY 1 9 2001		
JUN 0 6 2001		
JUL 2 8 2001		
AUG 3 8 2001		
SEP 2 5 2001		
NOV 1 8 2001		
FEB 1 9 2002		
SEP 3 0 2002		
NOV 2002		
2003		

PRINTED IN U.S.A.

CARING

Written by Shelagh Canning
Illustrated by Barbara Lanza

ROURKE, BOOK CO. INC.
VERO BEACH, FL 32964

Library of Congress Cataloging-in-Publication Data

Canning, Shelagh.
    Caring / Shelagh Canning.
       p.   cm. — (Doing the right thing)
Summary: Pictures and simple text show different ways of being helpful and showing that you care.
    ISBN 1-55916-235-X
     1. Helping behavior—Juvenile literature. [1. Caring.   2. Helpfulness.]
I. Title.   II. Series.
BF637.H4C36   1999
177'.7—dc21
                                        98-48389
                                            CIP
                                          AC

CARING

Caring is showing your love
for your family and friends.

4

Caring means helping a friend in trouble.

Caring is feeding your baby sister when
Mom is busy fixing dinner.

Show Dad you care. Help out with the
yard work so he can relax on his day off
from work.

Do not forget that you promised to
take care of your pet, rain or shine.

Caring is giving everyone a chance
to be part of the game.

Be sure to take care of the little
girl going trick-or-treating on
Halloween for the first time. She
may be shy or a little frightened.

Instead of buying a present for your
grandmother's birthday, show her how
much you care by fixing up her garden.

14

Caring is helping your sister learn
her part in the school play.

Take the time to show a special friend
you care.

17

Caring is sharing your good times
with older friends.

You care about your kitten, so you will ask
an adult to help you solve a problem with
your kitten that you cannot solve yourself.

Picking up your clothes to save your
mother extra work will show her that
you care about her.

21

The soccer coach cares about his players and wants them to have a good time. He treats his team to pizza when the game is rained out.

Your mom was very busy during her trip, but she cared enough to bring you a special gift.

Some people show they care by helping
neighbors with jobs the neighbors cannot
do by themselves.

It does not look as if your team has a
chance to win the game. Still, you cheer
them on. You care about your friends,
not about winning or losing.

Caring is giving money to those who do not have as much as you.

Your dad shows he cares when he takes you and your friends on a camping trip.

Accidents happen every now and then.
Caring means forgiving someone when
she says, she is sorry.

You know how much people care for you
because of what they do for you. You do
not always have to tell them you care.
Showing them you care is just as nice.

You Can Care for Others!

These steps can help you be caring. But do NOT write in this book; use a sheet a paper.

1. Choose ways you can show caring. Write 6 ways.

> Set the dinner table and put away dishes.
> Feed my pet on time every time.
> Don't laugh at someone who's different.
> Take part in a walkathon fund raiser.
> Tell Sis you are proud of her—in public.
> Think about words before you say them.

2. Choose who you can care for. Who cares for you? Who needs care? Write 6 real names.

brother	mom	grandfather	teacher
cousin	neighbor	buddy	pet

3. Choose how to care for each person. After each name, write a way to be caring. Use your list or think of new ways.

Think before speaking	kids in my class
Walk in a walkathon	child in hospital
Feed my pet	Lucky, my dog
Carry groceries to kitchen	Mom and Dad

4. Choose to start now. Show someone you care before you go to bed tonight.

5. Choose to show caring each day. Think about caring soon after you get out of bed.

6. Write these words every evening:
   Today I showed _____ I care by _____.
Fill in the blanks. Use the same paper every time. Keep it up for 2 weeks.

7. Say, "I care. And I show it."
   Say it many times every day.